Stressed Out!!!

by

Dr. Mary L. Reed (Gates), CNHP, MH, ND

authorHOUSE

1663 Liberty Drive, Suite 200
Bloomington, Indiana 47403
(800) 839-8640
www.authorhouse.com

First published by AuthorHouse 01/17/05

ISBN: 1-4184-7013-9 (e)
ISBN: 1-4184-7681-1 (sc)

Printed in the United States of America
Bloomington, Indiana

This book is printed on acid-free paper.

For more information on health go to:
http://www.MarysHerbs.com
or email: MarysHerbs@aol.com

Clinical Study: http://www.OCD-Free.org

Table of Contents

Introduction

There are so many books that I have read by someone who believes he or she has discovered "THE Cure" for a certain disease.

For instance Cancer..... One author says that "ALL cancers are caused by parasites" , another says "ALL cancers are caused by stress", yet another says "THE cause is a hiatal hernia", some say "that the chemicals in our food is THE cause of cancer"; others are convinced that "pH imbalance is THE source".

What I think is that sometimes cancer may be caused by parasites, stress, hiatal hernia, chemicals, pH imbalance and/ or diet.

This book is not an "I found the absolute cure" book. Rather it explores a link between a thin myelin sheathing on the nerves and health conditions such as: ADD, OCD, Phobias, Panic Attacks, MS, Parkinson's, Bell's Palsy, Shingles, Mood Swings, Body Dysmorphia, Schizophrenia, Depression etc.

The fact is that not all people with thin myelin sheathing will get one of these conditions, nor does every person who has these conditions have a thin myelin sheathing. But, I have worked with helping others who have had a thin myelin sheathing and the conditions listed above. They then nourished their myelin, and for the vast majority of them symptoms of these conditions improved or totally disappeared. If the suggestions in this book do not help, then please look beyond this information.

I have written this book straight-forward and simply - in plain English rather than scientific language. Its purpose is to inform in a way that can be easily understood and easily read. I see no reason in baffling the reader with uncommon terms to impress them, if they have no idea what I am talking about.

Anatomy and Physiology of the Nervous System

Before going into details about health conditions, it is vital that you understand the anatomy (what it looks like) and physiology (how it works) of the nervous system and myelin sheathing.

The nerve can be compared to a copper wire, which carries an electrical impulse. The nerve transports electrical impulses from the brain to the tissues and back again.

The myelin sheathing of the nervous system can be compared to the plastic coating on the outside of a copper wire.

Copper wire

Plastic coating

The Nerve
(Axon)   The Myelin Sheathing Coating

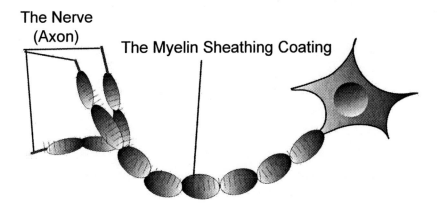

Dr. Mary L. Reed (Gates), CNHP, MH, ND

Functions of Myelin:

Myelin is a fatty substance which coats and protects the axon of the nerve (cells) from viruses such as the ones which cause Shingles and Bell's Palsy. If the myelin is healthy and thick enough, the virus cannot get to the actual nerve and cause symptoms of these conditions.

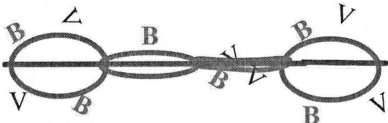

When the Myelin Sheathing is thin, Viruses and Bacteria can penetrate to the nerve causing the symptoms of conditions such as Bell's Palsy or Shingles.

Another function of the myelin is filtering, which can be best understood if you have ever turned on a CB Radio. You initially get all the background noise, static, etc., which can be quite nerve wracking. As you adjust the squelch button to filter out the background noise, you can hone in on the voices. The myelin acts as a type of squelching. It helps filter things out so you can concentrate on one thing at a time.

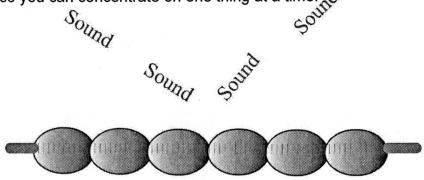

When your nervous system is unable to filter out the background noise, commotion and people get on your nerves easily. Loud sounds may startle or irritate you; some say it almost hurts.

If it is hard to concentrate (squelch out sound) when things are going on around you, it is often called ADD (Attention Deficit Disorder).

The myelin sheathing filters out sounds; it is important when sleeping; you can sleep through dull noises. Often, people with thin myelin have a hard time sleeping, so sounds wake them up. If you have a thin myelin sheathing, running the air conditioner or fan may help you sleep because of the constant sound. This constant sound (sometimes called white noise) helps keep a barking dog or your partner's snoring or grunting from waking you.

The myelin should also help the body shut off thoughts from the brain. If you have a hard time going to sleep because you can't seem to shut your mind off, suspect thin myelin.

I have had clients with thin myelin with whom I have worked say that they would have invasive thoughts of violence or immorality. This often disturbs them, because they consider themselves very moral and gentle people.

You do not have to have all of the above symptoms to have a thin myelin. (Refer to the test on pages 4 - 6).

	Never	Seldom	Often	Always
Do noises, people or commotion get on your nerves? Many people control it. I don't mean do you react to it negatively, but does it bother you?				
Do you avoid large groups of people or noisy places?				
Do you have a hard time concentrating when things are going on around you?				
Do you tend to turn things off or down when someone talks to you?				
Do you have a hard time getting to sleep?				
Do you have invasive thoughts at night?				
Do you play the radio, TV, fan, or air conditioner to help you sleep better or to help you fall asleep?				
Do sudden noises startle you?				
Do you have a hard time shutting your mind off at night to go to sleep?				

	Never	Seldom	Often	Always
Less than 6 days a week, do you dream vividly and remember the dream for about 20 minutes after you awaken?				
Do you catch yourself double checking things?				
Do you have rituals that you need to do to feel you did something right?				
Do you ever think you see someone or something out of the corner of your eye, but when you turn your head, nothing is there?				
Do you ever hear voices that are not there?				
Do you ever hear music or sounds that are not there?				
Do you ever feel that someone is next to you, but no one is there?				
Do you have to say your prayers over and over again because you fear you didn't say them right				

	Never	Seldom	Often	Always
Do you forget where you are or what direction a place is that you have gone often?				
Do you ever forget common words?				
Do you ever do something that is routine and suddenly wonder if you did it wrong?				
Do you ever forget common everyday information? For example, which side of a road barrier you should drive on.				
Do you ever worry that you have caused injury to someone (even if you didn't see anyone) and have to check to make sure you didn't?				

If you choose "Never" do not give yourself any point.

If you chose "Seldom" for any question, give yourself 1 point.

If you choose "Often" for any question, give yourself 2 points.

If you choose "Always" for any question give yourself 3 points.

The number of points indicate the possibility of the following:

0- 6 points - Better than average healthy myelin sheathing.

7- 12 points – Average myelin sheathing.

13 - 19 points - Thin myelin sheathing.

20 - 32 points - Very thin myelin sheathing.

33 - 66 points - Myelin sheathing in a desperate state.

There are exceptions to every rule and every test; this one is no different, but it seems quite accurate in helping someone determine if building their myelin sheathing would be beneficial to them in trying to overcome any symptoms stemming from:

Anorexia	Bell's Palsy
Bi-polarity	Body Dysmorphia
Bulimia	OCD
MS (Multiple Sclerosis)	Depression
Parkinson's disease	Self Injury or Self Cutting
Shingles	Social Phobia /Panic Attacks
Tourette's Syndrome	Trichotillomania, and other neurological disorders

The myelin also releases neurotransmitters.

A neurotransmitter is a substance that chemically connects one nerve ganglia impulse to another ganglia. Let me put it in easier terms.

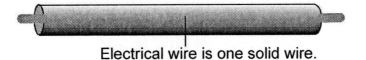

Electrical wire is one solid wire.

Unlike a copper wire, the nervous system is made up of sectioned nerves as seen below.

Nervous System is segmented

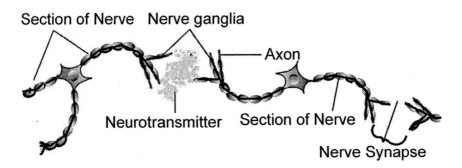

Section of Nerve Nerve ganglia

Axon

Neurotransmitter Section of Nerve

Nerve Synapse

The brain releases an electrical impulse. It travels down the nerve section to the ganglia, and the axon releases a chemical (neurotransmitter).

The adjacent nerve ganglia then draws in the neurotransmitter and that electric impulse continues to the next ganglia, etc.

The last section of nerve should receive the exact impulse that traveled the first sections of nerve.

Messages return to the brain in the same fashion.

For example, you decide to turn off the burner, the brain sends an electrical signal through this process and when it gets to the hand, your muscles move so your hand turns off the burner.

Your nerves sense that you touched it and the nerve impulse goes back and you get the sensation of touch. The message that the burner has been turned off is then relayed to the brain.

It is the axon which releases the neurotransmitters. But the potential for the amount of the neurotransmitter released is determined by the myelin.

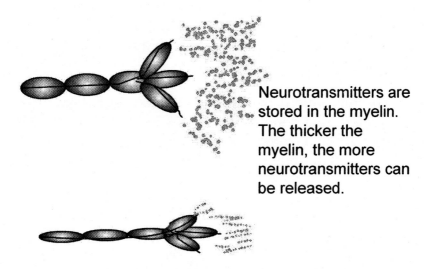

Neurotransmitters are stored in the myelin. The thicker the myelin, the more neurotransmitters can be released.

When the myelin is too thin, an inadequate amount of neurotransmitters are released.

Sometimes the myelin inhibits the ability of the axon to release enough of the neurotransmitters and the message that the burner has been turned off is dulled to the subconscious. It sends the message repeatedly that the burner needs turned off. Although you consciously know the burner is turned off, you feel compelled to turn it off again and again. This can be the foundation of the condition called Obsessive Compulsive Disorder (OCD).

This whole process of messages going to and from the brain is almost instantaneous. To understand how fast the whole process is, think of when you touch a hot pan. The sensation of pain starts at the nerve endings and the message is sent up the nerve chain until the information is perceived by the brain. The brain then processes the message and sends it back down the nerve chain, telling the muscles to remove your hand. This whole process can happen in a split second.

The brain and nervous system also perceive emotions. A signal created by a gentle caress goes to the brain, and the impulse produces a pleasant sensation. The same sensation may occur with a song, a taste, a color, or the warmth of sunlight.

One of the neurotransmitters is Serotonin. If an inadequate amount of neurotransmitters is available, the emotional state of the person will be affected. They will lack a feeling of well-being. When the myelin is too thin, the nerve axon may not be able to release enough of this chemical to give you a feeling of well being.

Drug companies have developed a line of drugs they call Selective Serotonin Reuptake Inhibitors (SSRI's).

To understand this, let me explain what ReUptake means.

After the nerve ganglia releases the chemical at the synapse and the adjoining nerve ganglia draws in this neurotransmitter and sends the electrical impulse on, the body then cleans out the excess that has not been drawn in.

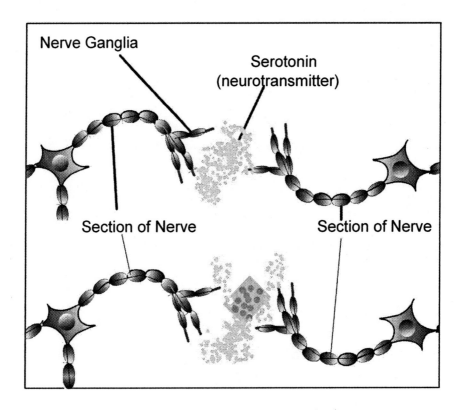

Think of reuptaking as a sponge which soaks up a spill. The process of reuptake is the body's way of cleansing the synapse after the impulse has passed through that section of the nerve.

Of course the body doesn't have little sponges. This is only an analogy of what happens.

Selective Serotonin Reuptake Inhibitors prevent the body from cleaning the Serotonin out of the synapse in between impulses. Some residue is left, hoping that the next impulse can mingle with what is there to try to compensate for the axon's inability to release enough.

If you are on a Selective Reuptake Inhibitor, DO NOT stop it. There will be a serious decrease in the availability of Serotonin, and you can become suicidal or homicidal.

Since St. John's Wort encourages the release of Serotonin, do not take it with SSRI's (Serotonin Reuptake Inhibitors).

Although the theory of this drug makes some sense, I believe we know so little about how the body works (even though the medical and science community has done a remarkable job at trying to understand), that whenever possible, we shouldn't interfere with the natural functions of the body.

For one thing many who come to me on these drugs say that their feelings seem "dulled" or "muddled". I believe this can be explained. I have no proof in this; it is just a strain of unscientific thought, like common sense.

Different emotions release different amounts and combinations of neurotransmitters. If the residue of a chemical that is released by an emotion mixes with the next set of chemicals, doesn't it make sense that the impulses or emotions involved would be effected?

I personally believe in trying to correct what is not functioning properly in the body rather than chemically altering it or working for the body. Therefore, I suggest to those who come to me to try to build up the health of the myelin and when they feel they do not need the Selective Serotonin Reuptake inhibitor, I suggest they ask their doctors to wean them off of it slowly. This should be done only under a doctor's care. (I do not say this to pacify the Medical Profession or keep my butt out of jail. I really believe it is the wisest course).

Some common Selective Serotonin Reuptake inhibitors are:

Fluoxetine HCL (Prozac), Sertraline HCL (Zoloft), Venlafaxine HCL (Effera), Parosetine HCL (Paxil).

The body's ability to heal is amazing. On a daily basis, I am in awe of what people have overcome when they give the body the needed materials.

It takes a long time to see a significant difference in the symptoms when working with rebuilding the myelin, but those who have, say it is well worth it.

Let's explore what the body needs to keep the nervous system healthy.

What erodes the cells of myelin?

STRESS

Probably one of the hardest things on the nervous system is Stress. We often say, " Man, am I stressed!" and laugh and shrug it off.

Stress causes many adverse reactions in the body. It plays havoc on the myelin. Some of this is because B Vitamins are water soluble and are washed out of the body easily during stressful times.

Unreleased stess seems to be the worst. I often encourage people to take up tiabo or aerobics to release the stress. Even punch a pillow. We teach our kids to hold in frustration. We teach them it is wrong to get angry, this is incorrect. Punching someone out is wrong, but everyone needs a safe outlet for stress; otherwise it will have a harmful effect on the body.

COFFEE, TEA and CAFFEINE

Coffee, tea and caffeine wash out B Vitamins and overstimulate the adrenals. It has been my experience that if you want to work on your nervous system and don't quit these, the progress is extremely slow or there is no progress.

LACK OF FATTY ACIDS

We are taught that fat is bad. I agree that we should not saturate our diet with animal fats, but we need fatty acids.

The main substance which makes up the cells of the brain and the covering of the nervous system is made of fatty acids. To cut the fat completely out of the body is to rob the body's source of raw materials it needs to repair the brain and myelin.

Many people avoid all fats like a plague. It is my opinion that there are going to be many health concerns developing because of it. Plant sources of fatty acids such as Flaxseed Oil, Evening Primrose Oil, Borage Oil are preferred.

LIVER FUNCTION

When we ingest fats, it is the liver's function to break down the fats into Vitamin F or Fatty acids small enough so the body can use them.

In general about 1 out of 2 people who come to me have symptoms of a liver that is functioning at less than peak performance. That is easily understood with all the chemicals that are in our lives. (One of the liver's 561 known functions is to filter out chemicals).

There was a lady who came to me. Upon doing an Iridology analysis, I was concerned about her fatty acid availability. I asked her what her cholesterol was. She very proudly said, "It is excellent. It is a total of 130 with both HDL and LDL combined."

I was deeply concerned that her total cholesterol was so low, because the liver is supposed to produce cholesterol, and this was a sign that her liver was in distress.

Again, we are so frightened of high cholesterol that she felt secure because hers was so low.

I told her that with cholesterol that low and being on a fat-free diet, her brain and nerve function could soon be seriously impaired.

She gave me a blank stare and started to cry. I tried to calm her down and she said, "You don't understand, I am a nervous wreck, and the doctor told me that I have Alzheimer's."

Over the next 9 months we added fatty acids (plant source) and modified her diet, strengthened her liver, and her cholesterol increased to 190. She came to me absolutely radiant. She said "My life is so much sweeter, I am laid back like I use to be, and I have no symptoms of Alzheimer's. "
(note: Not all Alzheimer's suffers can be helped by fatty acids.)

That was around 1994. When I saw her a year ago (6 years later), she was still doing great!

LOUD NOISES

Often people who work in an environment where there is constant noise seem to have thin myelin. They get to the point that they tell me that sound almost hurts.

Whether this is from the sound or the vibration of the sound, I have no idea. (Remember that sound waves aka ultrasound or sonograms are used to break up kidney stones and gallstones). I am not sure of the causes of their deterioration.

ULTRASOUND (on fetus)

This brings a point that I would like to discuss. A colleague of mine is writing a book on the damage that ultrasound does to the fetus.

Although there is insufficient data on humans, there are at least 35 studies done on animals that have been published, and their reports demand more research.

Those who work with natural health often compare statistical trends to what is happening to the health of Americans. The increase of ultrasound is matched by that of the increase of Attention Deficit Disorder.

Doctors now routinely prescribe sonograms (ultrasound) for such routine data as: Estimation of gestational age; monitoring fetal growth; and later in the pregnancy, fetal position.

FACT: The standing position of the official review panel which determined the safety of ultrasound is: "That it should only be used to indicate prenatal morbidity (gross deformation) or mortality (death)."

The most recent review that was published was in 1984 where the Bureau of Radiological Health, the FDA, the World Health Organization and National Council on Radiation Protection and Measurements studied biological effects of ultrasound such as: Immune response, change in chromosomal abnormalities, free radical damage and cell/membrane change and death.

They suggested further study be done. They ended this section of their report with this quote: "The existence of these studies is one of the factors that contributed to our decision that routine ultrasound screening cannot be recommended at this time."

Doctors believe that statistics is an unscientific approach at analyzing cause and effect of health conditions.

Although following statistics cannot solely determine cause and effect, statistics also should not be ignored.

Still confused? Let me explain a little about ultrasound. This comes from an article by the Science Department of Duke University. Sound (including ultrasound) is a wave of pressure that needs to travel either through air or liquid. Without these mediums, there is no sound.

Sound is measured by its vibratory rate called Hertz (Hz), either kilo or mega. The higher the frequency, the shorter the wavelength.

It is difficult, if not impossible, to accurately measure high frequencies.

There was one quote from this article which deeply concerned me: "Under right conditions, irradiation of a liquid with ultrasound leads to the formation and collapse of gas and vapor filled bubbles or cavities in the solution. The collapse of these bubbles can be violent enough to lead to interesting chemical effects."

After evaluating this information, if you ask me if I believe in ultrasound just as a routine during pregnancy I would have to be even more forceful than before when I say "DEFINITELY NOT".

The amazing part is that my strong opinion is from the research of the medical profession.. It was their own report that totally convinced me to avoid advocating ultrasound.

So many people say, "Well if it wasn't safe, then it would not be recommended by the AMA. Medical science does not, in my opinion, have a good track record. For instance, at one time x-ray treatments for enlarged tonsils were accepted as completely safe, I have a cousin who developed thyroid cancer years after her x-ray treatments. It was discovered that those treatments predisposed many of its victims to cancer. So just because it is accepted, it does not necessarily make it safe.

What is in the future for children who had been the fetus that had the ultrasound aimed at him or her?

What is even more scary is that the statements which are made are not stating that ultrasound is safe but saying the lack of risk is ASSUMED.

VIRUS or BACTERIA or PARASITE

There is a theory that a virus can attack the myelin as in Multiple Sclerosis (which has other causes). This is one which I have not explored and feel it is a lifetime's work in itself. There is a lot of speculation that MS is caused by something either viral, bacterial or parasitic from a cat.

TOXICITY

There is another theory that a toxic bowel can cause an auto-immune disease.

The body absorbs nutrients from the bowel. There is a theory that when nutrients from a toxic bowel are absorbed, toxins are absorbed with the nutrients. The cells of the sheathing are made of materials which contain toxic material.

The immune system knows that the cells are inferior and will attack them, destroying them so they can be replaced. If all the nutrients are toxic because of chronic toxic bowel, the replaced cells will also be toxic; therefore, the immune system never slows down in tearing down the myelin.

This vicious cycle can be one of the causes of auto-immune disease.

Dr. Mary L. Reed (Gates), CNHP, MH, ND

pH IMBALANCE

Through Iridology, I see that there is a relationship between the health of the myelin and the pH of the body. We in America eat a diet that is too processed and imbalanced. I suggest a book called YOUR HEALTH YOUR CHOICE by Dr. Ted Morter that can help you develop a diet that is balanced.

Since the first edition of this book, I have learned how a pH imbalance can prevent the cells from absorbing certain nutrients. Therefore, I suggest to test for a pH imbalance, and if one exists, to correct it by going on a pH balanced diet.

This consists mostly of cutting out coffee, tea, soda, and milk products, limiting starches and proteins and increasing raw and sweet fruits and raw vegetables.

There are other minor things which tear down the myelin sheathing, but these are the most common.

Improving the health of the myelin.

If you were to build or repair a room, you would need certain things.

You would need a blue print, construction workers, boards, hammers, nails, etc.

The same holds true if you want to repair or build the health of the body (including the myelin sheathing).

First you will need a blue print. DNA - (deoxyribonucleic acid) is like a blue print. It is drawn up and established before birth. Throughout your life, your body's systems try to maintain the specifications of this blueprint.

The model of DNA (as pictured on the previous page) looks much like a twisted ladder. If you didn't have a health condition at birth, then it is not in your DNA or blue print and theoretically you should be able to reverse conditions which develop later on by giving the body what it needs to repair.

The human body starts out as a sperm and an egg. And with no outside prompting, it grows into a human being. This self motivated mechanism stays with you and is what heals your body when there is an injury or sickness.

If something gets in its way or if it is lacking the proper raw building materials, it will not be able to keep up the specifications.

RNA - (ribonucleic acid) could be compared to construction workers which implement the blue print (DNA).

The more construction workers the faster the building. The more RNA available the faster the body's health can be rebuilt.

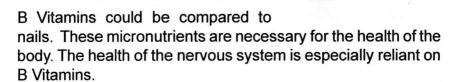

The RNA helps the body replace inferior cells. Spirulina helps increase the availability of the RNA. It appears to speed up the healing process of the nervous system.

B Vitamins could be compared to nails. These micronutrients are necessary for the health of the body. The health of the nervous system is especially reliant on B Vitamins.

Although there are foods which contain B vitamins, the body should be able to manufacture most of your B vitamins. There should be bacteria in the intestine (called acidophilus, bifodophilus, etc.) that basically eats (yeast) and excretes (poops out) B-Vitamins.

Antibiotics kill off the bacteria in the intestine. Those who have taken large amounts of antibiotics, more likely than not don't have enough of this bacteria.

Those who eat a diet high in commercially raised meat, might be ingesting the fat soluble antibiotics used on the animals. causing a similar imbalance caused by lack of the friendly bacteria.

 A book that I usually recommend on this subject is THE YEAST CONNECTION by Dr. Crook.

Vitamin B supplements are best taken as a combination of the complex of B vitamins.

Common symptoms of a Vitamin B deficiency are: Sunlight bothering your eyes, dry eyes, cracks at the corner of your mouth, the restless leg syndrome (rhythmically jiggling your leg), irritability, and muscle twitches.

Continuing the analogy of building or repairing a room, think of the fatty acids like the boards of the myelin. It is the number one building block of the myelin.

The main reasons for a lack of fatty acids are: a diet insufficient of fatty acids, which is a growing condition since people have been taught to be so afraid of fats. and a liver which is unable to break fats down into a useable size of fatty acids.

Flaxseed oil, borage oil and evening primrose oil which are fatty acids from plant source are preferred over the animal fats. As a rule of thumb, I suggest 2 Flaxseed capsules for every 10 to 15 pounds (not to exceed 32 capsules a day) OR 1 Evening Primrose oil for every 12 to 17 pounds daily (not to exceed 15 a day) .

It takes time to build a house. The body has a set time in which it slows down other functions so it can concentrate on healing the body. The time is when you are sleeping. You need an adequate amount of sleep to heal and build.. Often when someone has been sick or in an accident or after an operation, they sleep a lot. The body induces the sleep so it can concentrate on healing.

Without adequate amount of good sleep the body can not heal efficiently.

An indication that you are in a good level of sleep (also known as the 4th level of sleep or REM) is dreaming.

Dreaming means that your body has the nutrients it needs to get into the level of sleep where you can heal efficiently.

It is therefore important to get into the right level sleep (REM) and get the amount of sleep needed. You wouldn't expect your house to be built quickly if you limit the time you allow the construction workers to build.

You can't expect you body to heal if you limit the amount of sleep you get.

Often when people start on Nervine herbs such as Scullcap, Valerian, Lobelia, Catnip, Passion flower etc. initially it makes them drowsy. Often this levels out after a week or so.

What seems to happen is the body having the herbs to heal will induce the sleep so it can heal. Usually after the body is use to these nutrients, it will not induce sleep except at night.

Dr. Mary L. Reed (Gates), CNHP, MH, ND

I believe nervine herbal combination work so much better than single herbs. Some will be suggested later on.

It is absolutely amazing what the human body can overcome when it has the right raw materials. In the following pages are different health conditions and what might be achieved when the regimens are followed.

NOTE: It may take months to years of supplementation to rebuild the myelin.

Part II

Making the connection between nerve health and health conditions.

The functions of the myelin and the symptoms of a thin myelin are not commonly connected.

Let's examine health conditions, accompanying symptoms and some of the functions of the myelin a bit closer.

The myelin helps you filter out noise and commotion.

ADD

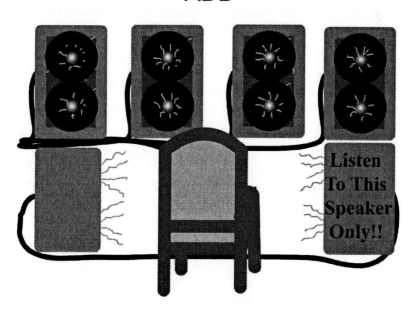

Imagine sitting in a chair surrounded by speakers. Each speaker is playing a different radio station and none of the speakers could be turned down.

Remembering that the myelin helps you filter out sounds or commotion, can you imagine how difficult it would be to concentrate on the one speaker only? A thin myelin prevents the ability to tune out sounds.

They would all hit you with equal intensity. The other speakers would easily distract you. People who are easily distracted are often labeled as having ADD (Attention Deficit Disorder)

ADD is running rampant. A friend of mine, who is a school nurse, said it is unbelievable how many children line up every day for her to administer Ritalin. It takes her both lunch hours just to administer it.

Knowing that building the myelin of the nervous system can help the symptoms of ADD, It makes me cringe when someone puts their child on Ritalin, because, before I knew about herbs, I had put my son on Ritalin and it almost destroyed his liver.

From those with whom I have worked, I would estimate that about one third of all those who have faithfully tried to improve the health of their myelin report the symptoms of ADD improve dramatically. They tell me how much easier it is to concentrate.

They tell me that their thoughts are not as scattered. When they start a task they finish it without jumping to something else.

Many people say that they used to work all day, but didn't get much done. For instance, they might start doing the dishes and notice the towels need folded and stop in the middle of the dishes to fold the towels, then they remember the wash should be done and sort the clothes, and before they put it in realize the detergent is low, so they took a shower to go shopping.

After they nourished the myelin, they noticed they could complete a task and not get distracted.

Bell's Palsy or Shingles
(When a virus attacks the nerve)

As stated before, one of the functions of the myelin is to protect the nerve. When the myelin is healthy, a virus has a harder time getting to the nerve.

I always suspect a thin myelin when someone has suffered from Bell's Palsy (a swelling of the nerve causing weakness or sagging of the muscles in the face) or Shingles (pain and blistering which scabs over, running the length of a nerve). After all, if the myelin was healthy, how could the virus get to the nerve?

Both of these conditions typically last months to even a year or more, but to date when people have taken VS-C and L-Lysine, they have not had the symptoms for longer than 1 week.

I usually suggest aggressive amounts of those herbs .... VS-C (a Chinese viral combination - 1 capsule for every 6 to 8 pounds of body weight a day) and L-lysine (an amino acid - 4 to 6 a day).

After the symptoms are gone, I always suggest they build the myelin sheathing to avoid reoccurrence. The two viruses that cause Bell's and Shingles can lay dormant in the body for years.

The virus can become active again during times of stress or when the immune system has been compromised. It is not uncommon to go through several bouts of the same condition.

Dr. Mary L. Reed (Gates), CNHP, MH, ND

Anxiety, Panic Attacks, Phobias, Social Anxiety Disorders, etc.

I have grouped these together because the symptoms are quite close. Panic, anxiety and phobias are felt more strongly by the sufferer than the situation would invoke in the average person.

Besides soothing the nerve, the myelin helps in the release of serotonin. Many people who have anxiety, panic attacks, phobias social anxiety disorder, etc., often notice a difference when they take serotonin reuptake inhibitors, which would strongly indicate a thin myelin.

Often these are considered psychological (mental) rather than physiological (physical). I totally disagree. If it were psychological only, why would administering SSRI drugs help these conditions?

Another indicator that they are physiological is that those who have the anxiety, panic, etc., often have accompanying symptoms of thin myelin. They usually respond very well over a long-term program focusing on improving the health of the sheathing of the nerve.

I often suggest a quick but temporary fix, because this feeling can become overwhelming and the herbs can take a long time to see significant improvements (often several months). Distress remedy and Tahitian Noni seem to help sufferers cope during this process.

Schizophrenia

(Loss of reality, paranoia often accompanied by visual and audio hallucination.)

Schizophrenia is also considered by most to be totally psychological. This might be true for some, but I have seen people stop hallucinating when they have taken herbs to nutritionally support the nervous system.

The intensity of the symptoms of those who have been helped, are usually very subtle, like seeing movement, shadow or someone standing in their peripheral (out the side of the eye) vision.

People have told me they felt someone standing near them or sitting down next to them and when they look no one is there.

Some also report that they hear someone call their name or hear music or something in the distance, which is not there.

They are totally functioning in the world. As a matter of fact, when I first mention it, many have giggled nervously and when they feel comfortable, affirm that they experience this.

Sometimes they burst out in tears because they feared they were going crazy and afraid to tell anyone.

These mild symptoms of schizophrenia respond very well with the program to build the myelin sheathing. Of course it is always a possibility this condition is caused by a deficiency, which is satisfied when trying to nourish the nerves. Most do not care which it is, they are just glad the hallucinations are gone.

29

Dr. Mary L. Reed (Gates), CNHP, MH, ND

Neuropathy (non-diabetic)

Disruption in the nerve health

Neuropathy causes numbness and pain of the nerves.

I would like to make brief mention of neuropathy. Although it is best for the sufferer to work with the health of the myelin, I usually suggest castor oil topically when it affects the feet.

I am not sure exactly how it works, but it seems to produce dramatic results in many people.

OCD
Obsessive Compulsive Disorder

OCD is defined as a neurotic (severe depression and anxiety) condition characterized by persistent unwanted thoughts and/or repeated, ritualistic behavior.

Basically you check or think about things over and over again. I believe this to be caused by thin myelin sheathing.

This is my theory of what happens...

Let us take for example, deciding to lock the door. The brain releases an electrical impulse to lock the door. The impulse goes to the synapse, where a chemical (neurotransmitter) is released.

The next nerve ganglia draws it up, which travels down the nerve chain until it gets to the muscle in the hand and the hand locks the door.

When the hand has locked the door, an impulse goes from the hand up the nerve chain to tell the brain the mission is accomplished.

If the myelin is too thin, it is not able to release enough of the neurotransmitters to get the "mission accomplished" impulse back to the brain.

If the neurotransmitters are released less than 100% between each ganglia, the impulse may be dulled or fade away.

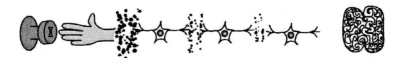

Although consciously the person knows they have locked the door, their subconscious is not sure, so the brain sends out the signal again to lock the door.

Since the brain is not getting all the input of what the body is doing, it has a difficult time. Fears and uncertainties might develop.

The favored conventional treatment for OCD is behavior modification. I truly believe this is not just a bad habit someone has developed.

Many people who start the symptoms of OCD, trace it to stress and forgetting to do something which puts undue emphasis on that task. I believe emphasizing the behavior might cause as many problems as it will help.

Health Vs Disease

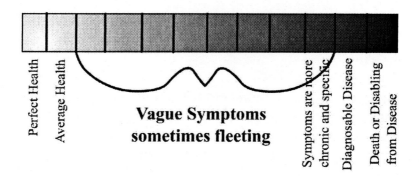

Perfect Health

Average Health

Vague Symptoms sometimes fleeting

Symptoms are more chronic and specific

Diagnosable Disease

Death or Disabling from Disease

Many people believe you are either healthy or you have a disease and the distance between the two is narrow. This is not so. Your body is not healthy one day and diseased the next.

There is a wide band between Health and Disease. The following chart illustrates more closely, the progression of disease.

MS (Multiple Sclerosis) and Parkinson's disease are diseases of the nervous system. Often people can remember back to vague symptoms years before they were diagnosed or diagnosable.

Medical tests are designed to diagnose Disease and do not measure Health.

I believe in working with a toxin or deficiency as soon as it starts to produce any symptoms. It is through seemingly unrelated symptoms that I try to find signs of deficiencies which need balanced out.

This kind of "Stitch in Time Saves Nine" approach, I believe can ward off disease before it ever starts.

Suggesting an Herbal Program

On the following pages are guidelines to help you determine what nutrients your nervous system may need in order to be healthy.

Answering yes to more than 3 questions on pages 4 thru 6 indicates you may benefit from taking the foundation herbs of Flaxseed Oil (or Evening Primrose Oil) and Spirulina. I would then build on the program, adding other herbs as the symptoms would indicate.

SYMPTOM	SUGGESTED SUPPLEMENT
If you catch yourself double checking things and you have an average reaction to stimulants or depressants, for example caffeine keeping you awake.	Nerve Control (RE-X) *
If you see things out of the corner of your eye like movement or shadows.	Chinese Stress Relief (STR-C) *
If you have a really hard time falling asleep.	Herbal Sleep *
If you are under 16, unless you react the opposite to stimulants and depressants.	Stress Relief (STR-J) *
Restless legs, sunlight bothering your eyes, dry eyes.	B-COMPLEX
Have a lack of Dopamine (L-Dopa)	Velvet Bean

I suggest start taking the amount suggested on the bottle and increase until you dream nightly and remember those dreams for approximately 20 min after you wake up. After a period of time you can decrease but keep using dreaming nightly as your guide to do so.

SYMPTOMS	SUGGESTED SUPPLEMENT	SUGGESTED AMOUNT
If you have all of the following: Eczema, Hair loss, Constipation (for children do under the supervision of a competent professional)	Inositol	1 Gram per every 15 - 20 pounds (don't exceed 14 gram a day)
If there is inflammation of the nerves	***Evening Primrose Oil	1 capsule for every 12 – 15 pounds (not to exceed 15 a day)
If there doesn't seem to be inflammation	***Flaxseed Oil	2 capsules for every 10-15 pounds (not to exceed 32 a day)
If you have any symptoms which indicate a weak liver, such as: Bloating or gassiness more than 1 times a week. Sluggish bowels, less than 2 times a day. Waking up during the night. Blood sugar imbalances. For females, heavy or clotty periods, tenderness of the breast or PMS	Liver Cleanse**	

SYMPTOMS	SUGGESTED SUPPLEMENT	SUGGESTED AMOUNT
Lack of ambition, thinning hair, weight gain (for women usually)	ProGYam 500	Depends on your hormone levels, age, balance and gender.
For those who are over 21	Spirulina	1 capsule per every 25 pounds
Lacking dopamine, Parkinson's those who have had success with Dopamine ReUptake Inhibitors	Black Velvet Bean	As recommended
pH imbalance, weak back, mucus, lack of muscle strength. (for adults only)	Skeletal Strength (SKL)	1 tablet per every 10 to 15 pound (not to exceed 12 a day)
pH imbalance, whining children, ear infections or mucus (for children only)	Calcium Magnesium with Vitamin D	1 tablet every 20 pounds (not to exceed over 12 a day)

**If your liver has all the nutrients it needs and is working efficiently you should sleep without waking up at night... not even to urinate. I would start with what is on the bottle and increase until you sleep all night without waking up.

*** All fat soluble supplements (such as Flaxseed Oil and Evening Primrose Oil), should be taken with a protein to help ensure the needed liver producing digestion to emulsify the fats so no liver damage is experienced.

The information above is just a suggested guideline. Every person is different. Learning to listen to what your body needs is very advantageous in regaining and maintaining its health.

A healthy diet comprised of raw vegetables, fruits, legumes, beans, and good water is a very good base for all health.

I work with herbs and herbal combinations which have no presently known interactions with any meds. However, you may want to ask your pharmacist for dietary or herbal restrictions if you are on meds.

Turkey is a source of L-tryptophan. This amino acid is the precursor of serotonin.

Case Study

Most health books mention case studies. For example, John D from Montana was cured of something. Although most of them are probably accurate and honest, I am a skeptic so I do not mention case studies throughout the book.

I am going to make one exception. It was this case that led me to make the connection between a thin myelin and some of the symptoms and health conditions discussed in this book.

The history of this case starts in 1979. She was 22 (years old) and had just escaped an extremely physically and emotionally abusive and stressful marriage. Then side effects of medication robbed her of her good health.

When she first started developing the symptoms on the questionnaire, she didn't tell people because she had two small children and thought she was going insane. She was afraid her children would be taken from her.

She would be introduced to and helped dramatically with Alternative Therapies. Herbs and nutrition helped her with the health of her kidneys, menses, thyroid and heart.

Although she did not have a name for the symptoms, she was experiencing at the time (21 years ago), the symptoms were typical of OCD and agoraphobia. So severe were her symptoms that she couldn't step outside her home for a little over 6 months.

Later on it was determined that she had a weak liver and thin myelin, she took LIV-A, RE-X (Now called Nerve Control), Evening Primrose Oil and Spirulina. She had no idea why her symptoms had started to go away.

Having most of her health restored profoundly affected her life and she studied to become a Natural Health Practitioner. She started to work with others and noticed that those who had a thin myelin experienced many of her old symptoms. When they took the herbs, their symptoms went away.

Since 1992 she has been totally free of her panic attacks, anxiety, OCD and Agoraphobia.

She then learned all she could about nutrition, anatomy/physiology and herbs and worked with thousands of people who experienced some of the same results.

Wanting to help others who had been stressed out to the point of ruining their lives, she decided to help others by writing a book called STRESSED OUT..

Yours in Good Health,

Dr. Mary L Reed (Gates), CNHP, MH, ND

Appendix A

Food pH

(80% alkaline.....20% acidic)

Most Alkaline	Alkaline	Lowest Alkaline	Food Category	Lowest Acid	Acid	Most Acidic
Lemons, Watermelon, Limes, Grapefruit (if not bitter), Mangoes, Papayas	Dates/Figs, Melons, Grapes, Papaya, Kiwi, Most Berries (if sweet), Apples, Pears, Raisins	Oranges(if sweet), Bananas, Cherries, Pineapple (if fully ripened), Peaches, Avocados	**FRUITS**	Plums, Processed fruit juices	Sour Cherries, Rhubarb	Blueberries, Cranberries, Prunes
Asparagus, Onions, Vegetable juices (fresh), Parsley, Raw Spinach, Broccoli, Garlic	Okra, Squash, Green Beans, Beets, Celery, Lettuce, Zucchini, Sweet Potato	Carrots, Tomatoes, Fresh Corn, Mushroom, Cabbage, Peas, Potato skins, Olives	**BEANS VEGGIES, LEGUMES**	Spinach, Kidney Beans, String Beans	Potatoes, Pinto Beans, Navy Beans, Lima Beans	Soybean, Carob

Most Alkaline	Alkaline	Lowest Alkaline	Food Category	Lowest Acid	Acid	Most Acid
			MEATS	Venison, Cold Water Fish	Turkey, Chicken, Lamb	Pork*, Beef, Shellfish*
		Amaranth, Millet, Wild Rice, Quinoa	**GRAINS CEREAL**	Sprouted Wheat Bread, Spelt, Brown Rice	White Rice, Corn, Buckwheat,	Wheat, White Flour*, Pastries*, Pasta
			GRAINS		Oats, Rye	
	Almonds	Chestnuts	**NUTS SEEDS**	Pumpkin seeds, Sunflower seeds	Pecans, Cashews	Walnuts, Peanuts*
	Breast Milk	Raw Goats milk, Goat Cheese, Whey	**EGGS DAIRY**	Eggs, Yogurt*, Buttermilk*, Cottage cheese*	Soy Cheese*, Cheese+, Raw Milk*, Soy milk+	Cheese*, Homogenized milk*, Ice cream*
Lemon Water, Herb teas		Ginger Tea	**BEVER-AGES**		Tea*, Coffee*	Beer*, Soft Drinks*
Olive Oil	Flax Oil	Canola oil*	**OILS**	Corn Oil+		
Stevia	Maple syrup, Rice syrup	Raw Honey, Raw Sugar	**SWEET-ENERS**	Processed honey, Molasses	White sugar*, Brown sugar	NutraSweet*, Equal*, Sweet 'N' Low*

41

Items marked with an "*" I believe should be cut out completely.

Items marked with a "+" I believe it is necessary to make sure source is not bioengineered (GMO –Genetically Modified).

(Modified chart of Dr. Theodore Baroody, Ph.D., N.D.). Your diet should be 80% alkalizing foods and only 20% acidic foods to maintain correct pH balance.

Appendix B

Premise #1

Myelin Sheathing Stores Neurotransmitters.

Premise #2

Symptoms of OCD, Depression, Bi-polar, Trichotillomania, Parkinson's, MS, Anorexia, Body Dysmorphia, Self Injury or Self Cutting, Panic Attacks, Social Phobia, Tourette's and other neurological disorders are often alleviated or lessened by SSRI's (Selective Serotonin ReUptake Inhibitor) or Dopamine ReUptake Inhibitor which tries to increase the availability of neurotransmitters.

Hypothesis

A thin myelin is the root of the conditions listed above. And improving the health of the myelin can help improve or possibly correct these conditions.

Data Gathered

On January 15, 2004, on our website http://www.OCD-Free. org, we gathered information via an automated questionnaire. This questionnaire evaluates symptoms of a thin myelin.
We gathered the info for exactly 2 months. The 29 participants were given a random computer generated User ID (to protect their privacy).

Break down of participants.

0 – Were Diagnosed but without Symptoms

2 – Had Symptoms but weren't Diagnosed

19 – Were both Diagnosed and had Symptoms

8 – Were neither Diagnosed nor had Symptoms

Represented by the chart below.

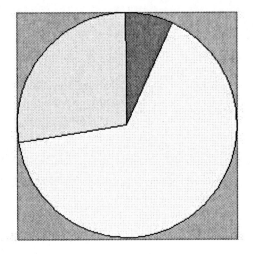

☐ Diagnosed Only

■ Symptoms Only

☐ Both Diagnosed and Symptoms

☐ Neither Diagnosed Nor Symptoms

There are many ways of interpreting data. Included is the Raw Data.

USER ID	SYMPTOMS ONLY	BOTH SYMPTOMS AND DIAGNOSED	NEITHER SYMPTOMS OR DIAGNOSED	SCORE
08F4206IR1				50
IAI26SGZ6A			X	41
23U626CV1B			X	49
2EOW18AD42		X		78
34HI7G63E8		X		88
3E0498IDTF		X		46
3II60FZY3R		X		44
42U44A204M		X		54
52UI8PD56M			X* not OCD but Anxiety Attacks, BPD and DID, Clinical Depression	58
6288IXC075		X		76
7474A1668			X	54
79HKM7PCMR			X	24
85JS7I63K0			X Anticipatory Anxiety, Depression	63
957Z1858NV		X		35
C7T5Y003B7		X		48
JPRU9K51RZ	X			46
TCBB34R21		X		47
JXWU708604		X		54
L1BA762V89		X		51
L25I666695		X		47
K60U7UG3Q		X		44
O644712S0S	X			50
P944973Y6		X		50
S4S4S236F		X		64
SE5N6GE812			X	46
SG9oX7C205				44
T66W09249B		X		39
YI985IBLK9		X		56

Summerized on the following page.

	Number of Participants	High Score Number	Low Score Number	Average Score Number
Those who have been diagnosed with OCD only	0	0	0	0
Those who have symptoms of OCD only	2	50	46	48
Those who have both symptoms of OCD and have been diagnosed with OCD	19	88	35	54.16
Those who have neither symptoms nor have the diagnosis of OCD.	8	63	24	47.88

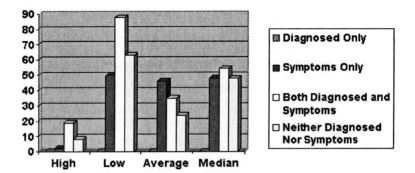

Toward the end of the first gathering of info, we added a place in the questionnaire which asks if any accompanying symptoms were being experienced. Symptoms such as anxiety, depression etc., were added in all the remaining questionnaires. All who filled it out who did not have OCD or symptoms did experience the conditions listed in the data below.

Taking that information into consideration would support the theory of a thin myelin even more. Included is the raw data for you to analyze for yourself.

Although the data we gathered isn't conclusive, I truly believe it indicates the theory is solid and warrants further study.

Dr. Mary L. Reed (Gates), CNHP, MH, ND

BIBLIOGRAPHY

Dr. Theodore Baroody ALKALIZE OR DIE,
Hills, Christopher, THE SECRETS OF SPIRULINA, University
of the Trees Press, Boulder Creek, CA 1980

Velma J. Keith and Monteen Gordon, THE HOW TO HERB
BOOK, Mayfield Publications, Pleasant Grove, UT 1991

Stephen Cherniske, CAFFEINE BLUES, Warner Books, New
York, NY, 1998

John W. Hole, Jr, Human Anatomy and Physiology, Web pub,
Pages 310-313, 320-331

Robert E. Rothenberg, M.D., F.A.C.S, The New Illustrated
Medical Encyclopedia and Guide to Family Health, Grolier
pub, Page 777

Frances Sizer and Eleanor Whitney, Nutrition Concepts and
Controversies, 7th Ed, West Wadsworth, Page 161-162

The Encyclopedia of Natural Remedies, Pages 191, 194, 195,
199, 213, 262

The Burton Goldberg Group, Alternative Medicine the Definitive
Guide, Future Medicine Publishing, Page 850

James F. Balch, MD, Phyllis A. Balch, CNC, Prescription for
Nutritional Healing, Avery, Page 131, 330

Janet Zand, LAc, OMD, Rachel Walton, RN, Bob Rountree,
MD, Smart Medicine for a Healthier Child, Avery, Page 221

Wynn Kapit/Lawrence M. Elson, The Anatomy Coloring Book,
Harper Collins, Page 11

Dr. Michael Colgan, The New Nutrition Medicine for the Millennium, CI Publications, Page 210-217

Michael T Murray, ND and Jade Beutler, RRT, RCP, Understanding Fat and Oils your Guide to Healing with Essential Fatty Acids, Apple Publishers, Page 41

DIAGNOSTIC ULTRASOUND IMAGING IN PREGNANCY,

National Institutes of Health Consensus Development Conference Statement, February 6-8, 1984 (can be viewed at:) http://text.nlm.nih.gov/nih/cdc/www/41txt.html#Head3

Editors of TIME LIFE, The Medical Advisor the Complete Guide to Alternative and Convential Treatments, TIME-LIFE Publishing, Page 603, 658-663

Dr. George Watson, Nutrition and Your Mind, Bantam 1978

Dr. Paul Holmon, OCOF:MT Waverly, Australia, Nov-Dec: 3-5, 1992, OC-51034

The Merck Manual of Medical Information, Pocket Books Health, Page 347

ABOUT THE AUTHOR

Mary L. Reed (Gates) is a Certified Natural Health Professional, Master Herbalist and Doctor of Naturopathy.

She is currently gathering information to help prove and fine tune her protocol via her website http://www.OCD-Free.org

She herself being symptom free from OCD since 1992, is dedicating the rest of her life, helping others become symptom free as well.

Printed in the United States
36441LVS00003B/226

9 781418 476816